Edward Bulwer Lytton, Julian Henry Charles Fane

Tannhäuser

The Battle of the Bards - A Poem

Edward Bulwer Lytton, Julian Henry Charles Fane

Tannhäuser
The Battle of the Bards - A Poem

ISBN/EAN: 9783744669825

Printed in Europe, USA, Canada, Australia, Japan

Cover: Foto ©Thomas Meinert / pixelio.de

More available books at **www.hansebooks.com**

TANNHÄUSER.

MOBILE, ALA.: PRINTED AT THE REGISTER & ADVERTISER BOOK AND JOB OFFICE

TANNHÄUSER;

OR,

The Battle of the Bards.

A Poem.

BY

NEVILLE TEMPLE, AND EDWARD TREVOR.

MOBILE:

PUBLISHED BY S. H. GOETZEL & CO., 33 DAUPHIN STREET.

1863.

THE reader is solicited to adopt the German pronunciation of TANNHÄUSER, by sounding

PUBLISHERS' NOTICE.

BEFORE going to press, with this admirable Poem, we esteem it our duty to express our sincere thanks to

WALKER FEARN, Esq.,

to whose great kindness we are indebted for a copy of the English edition.

At the same time we beg leave to call the attention of the reader to an able critique of the London Times, and have only to regret that we cannot avail ourselves of all the other criticisms, which appeared in all the English papers and periodicals, in praise of this extraordinary work of genius and art.

The names on the Title-page are only assumed; the authors in reality are, one a son of Bulwer, Secretary to the English Embassy at Vienna, and the other Julian Fano, the son of Lord Westmoreland.

MOBILE, ALA., February, 1863.

TANNHÄUSER.

When Dryden lay dying, he is said to have expressed deep regret and remorse for all the licentious and corrupt passages which defaced his noble writings. Convert to a faith which offers to the suffering soul the panacea of human absolution, he nevertheless groaned in spirit. Invested monarch of other men's minds by right of supreme ability, he died conscious that he had been an unfaithful ruler of his subjects. The words in which he made the tardy admission that authorship is a trust for which writers will be held accountable, are disputed. Johnson says that "his contemporaries, however they reverenced his genius, left his life unwritten, and nothing, therefore, can be known, beyond what casual mention and uncertain tradition have supplied." But the broad facts remain that, even in the loose and profligate age for which he wrote, he was virulently assailed for the extraordinary profligacy of his writings; that one of his comedies was prohibited after the third night, as too indecent for the stage; and that in his preface to his latest literary task, the *Fables*, while repelling the censures of Blackmore and Milbourne, and more especially of Collier, Dryden thus expresses himself:

"I have pleaded guilty to all thoughts or expressions of mine that can truly be accused of obscenity, immorality, or profaneness, and retract them. If he be my enemy, let him triumph; if he be my friend, he will be glad of my repentance."

That such a writer should need repentance for the legacy he bequeathed from the vanishing riches of his mind to his fellow-men, is a sorrowful thought; it is also an enduring lesson. It gives us, as the opinion of one of the greatest of departed writers, that the mastery of authorship is not to be prostituted, either for the mere earning of bread, the flattery of the great, or the pandering to the fluctuating taste of the public. If it is a trade, it should be an honest trade; if a power, a power loyally exercised; if a mere companionship of mind, a decent companionship.

The days of that excessive profligacy in writing are over. The great master Dryden, and the Congreves, and Vanbrughs, and Beaumonts, and Fletchers, whose license met no check in the diseased appetite of reckless applauders, have ceased to find imitators or successors. After them rose a divided empire of calm idealists and poets of passion and action; and after them the variety of schools belonging to the generation immediately preceding our own, when Byron and Scott, Moore and Wordsworth, Southey and Campbell, Crabbe and Coleridge, entranced, allured, or wooed attention in turn; when young gentlemen yearned to be Corsairs, with a Medora waiting for them in some island they didn't know where; or sang, in various keys, Anacreontic snatches by the reviver of Irish melodies; while the more serious dwelt thoughtfully on the graver pages of "the grey old man of Rydal Mount," who taught that

> "The soul that rises with us, our life's star,
> Hath had elsewhere its setting
> And cometh from afar;
> Not in entire forgetfulness,
> And not in utter nakedness,
> But trailing clouds of glory do we come
> From God, who is our home."

It is not too wild a boast to assert that among the writers of the generation now immediately present with us, something of the best of all the past, and nothing of the worst, abides, and satisfies at once the reason and the imagination. A school has risen up among us—moral in sentiment, passionate in diction, romantic in its themes—whose tranquil boast it well may be (whatever be its other defects), that its poetry cannot be read and pondered over by the young and enthusiastic without raising and purifying, instead of confusing and corrupting. It is not underrating the author of *The Corsair, Lara,* and *Parisina,* to say that the productions of this later school are a vast improvement on his rhymed romances; nor insulting even to the author of *Childe Harold,* to assume that an element is now introduced that would have enhanced the value even of that masterly production—the element of power for good over the minds of the young. The shadow and the glory that belonged to Milton flicker over the deep-toned strings of Tennyson's harp, leader of all the sounds of poetry in our land. Better than many sermons is the fine address which the Laureate puts into the mouth of his King Arthur to fallen Guinevere. Better than many lectures on fortitude is Longfellow's lovely exhortation to "suffer and be strong." Better than all the prosaic advice that could be given "to persons about to marry," the pure and simple picture of domestic life by the much-criticised Coventry Patmore; nor will those even who object to the peculiarities of a style combining much of the homeliness of Crabbe with sweeter music and a far higher range of thought, dispute the fact that a better landmark was set on the shores of time when Patmore published the poem entitled *The Angel in the House,* than when Moore took an obscure Scriptural text for his fabulous *Loves of the Angels,* or when the same theme furnished matter for Byron's semi-blasphemous *Heaven and Earth.*

The poem which stands for notice at the head of this article is indisputably "Tennysonian." It has been said that it is an imitation of Tennyson. If it were so, we might answer, "*Honi soit qui mal y pense.*" Wordsworth admitted that when he first began to write, he carefully studied Pope, for the express purpose of imitating him, and hoped he had done something "a little in his style." We must all write in the language of our country and of our time, and the greatest writers of that time will always exercise a special and varying control over the general rule which governs composition. *Tannhaeuser* belongs to the day in which Tennyson writes. Be it so. The orchestra music of our day is not that of Päer and Pasiello, but of Meyerbeer, and Verdi, and Mendelssohn. The music which lies hushed among our book leaves is Tennyson's. But as it is possible for each man to preserve his individuality though wearing a national costume, and speaking his land's language, so in these younger poets we perceive only general brotherhood, and no servile imitation. They have adhered to the fashion of blank verse established by Tennyson, whose matchless lyrics nevertheless prevent us from ranking him with those who hold that

> "—— barbarous nations, and more barbarous times,
> Debased the majesty of verse to rhymes;
> Those rude at first—a kind of hobbling prose
> That limped along and tinkled in the close."

They have preserved also the Tennysonian rule of the introduction of lyrics in the breaks of the blank verse. With the copying of these rules, and the echo here and there from well-known tones of thought in the great writer, all imitation ceases; and had the poem been published as Tennyson's, instead of with the modest assumption of unreal names, which seems another fashion of the day, we doubt (and we can pay the authors no higher compliment) if the public would have condemned the book as unworthy of his fame. Full of beauty of thought, melody of language, and sudden pictures that rise like visions before the reader, it is full also of noble and distinct morality. Indeed, the final touch of resemblance to Tennyson may be found in this; for many have painted the shame and despair of sin, but none ever painted the degradation from a happy height, the sorrowful "falling away" from better things, so well as that great master.

* The poem is founded on a German tradition, and represents the temptation of a young

knight lured from a pure attachment to the worship of the goddess Venus. Whether this be merely an allegory, and that Tannhäuser, during his absence from the Court of the Landgrave of Wartburg, was associated with "pretty horsebreakers," or whether he did abjure true religion for the mythological goddess, is left in obscurity. Meanwhile, nothing in modern poetry can be finer than the passage which describes the change from the gross worship paid to Sensualism:—

> "Till came the crack of that tremendous Doom
> That sent the false gods shivering from their seats,
> Shatter'd the superstitious dome that blear'd
> Heaven's face to man, and on the lurid world
> Let in effulgence of untainted light.
> As when, laid bare beneath the delver's toil
> On some huge bulk of buried masonry
> In hoar Assyria, suddenly reveal'd,
> A chamber, gay with sculpture and the pomp
> Of pictur'd tracery on its glowing walls,
> No sooner breathes the wholesome heavenly air
> Than fast its colored bravery fades, and fall
> Its ruin'd statues, crumbled from their crypts,
> And all its gauds grow dark at sight of day ;
> So darken'd and to dusky ruin fell
> The fleeting glories of a Pagan faith,
> Bared to Truth's influences bland, and smit
> Blind by the splendors of the Bethlehem Dawn."

Tannhäuser's maiden love is exquisitely described:

> "There came
> An evening with the Princess, when they twain
> Together ranged the terrace that o'erlaps
> The great south garden. All her simple hair
> A single sunbeam from the sleepy west
> O'erfloated ; swam her soft blue eyes suffused
> With tender ruth, and her meek face was moved
> To one slow, serious smile, that stole to find
> Its resting-place on his.
> "Then, while he looked
> On that pure loveliness, within himself
> He faintly felt a mystery like pure love :
> For through the arid hollows of a heart
> Sered by delirious dreams, the dewy sense
> Of innocent worship stole."

Unfortunately, this impression is not lasting, and wandering feverishly to the "horrid hill of Hoersel," where Venus dwells,

> "Bright in her baleful beauty he beheld
> The goddess of his dreams."

His meeting with Venus reminds us of a passage in another poem—too little known and too little read—Horne's "Orion;" and like Orion's meeting with Diana, it is fatal to his peace :

> "And, from that hour, in court,
> And chase, and tilted tourney, many a month,
> From mass in holy church, and mirth in hall,
> From all the fair assemblage of his peers,
> And all the feudatory festivals,
> Men missed Tannhaeuser."

And, as is still the custom in this busy world, missing him, they began to forget him ; only Elizabeth, his maiden love, still yearns after him :

> "One heart within that memory lived aloof,
> One face, remembering his, forgot to smile."

We will not spoil the pleasure of those who will read the book, by narrating at length how the excellent Landgrave wormed out of his niece the reason of her melancholy, or how, to dispel it, he summoned all the minstrel knights to improvise before her for the prize,

> "And hold high combat in the craft of song."

The absent Tannhäuser is fortunately met with in time to take his part in this " Battle of the Bards," for which purpose he re-appears among his former friends at Court. Here is a pleasant picture :

> " Shrill clink'd the corridors
> Through all the courts with clashing heels, or moved
> With silken murmurs, and elastic sounds
> Of lady laughters light ; as in they flow'd
> Lord, Liegeman, Peer, and Prince, and Paladin,
> And dame and damsel, clad in dimpling silk
> And gleaming pearl ; who, while the groaning roofs
> Re-echo'd royal music, swept adown
> The spacious hall, with due obeisance made
> To the high dais, and on glittering seats
> Dropp'd one by one, like flocks of burnished birds
> That settle down with sunset-painted plumes
> On gorgeous woods."

And this, when Tannhäuser bows before the dais where the Landgrave's niece is seated :

> " The Landgrave, at her side,
> Saw, as he mused what theme to give for song,
> The pallid forehead of Elizabeth
> Flush to the fair roots of her golden hair."

And willing, in his quality of uncle and chaperon, to give the Knight an opportunity of declaring his affection, from which he deems him withheld only by timidity, the worthy Landgrave proposes " Love" as the subject for improvisation.

So far, so good ; but to the amazement and horror of the courtiers, male and female, Tannhäuser bursts out in strains so passionately Anacreontic and improper, that the men, outraged at the insult offered to the fair sex present, draw their swords to slay the blasphemer then and there ; while the ladies take to flight :

> " Uprose on every side and rustled down
> The affrighted dames ; and, like the shuddering crowd
> Of particolour'd leaves that flits before
> The gust of mid October, all at once
> A hundred jewell'd shoulders, huddling, swept
> The halls, and slanted to the doors, and fled
> Before the storm, which now from shaggy brows
> 'Gan dart indignant lightnings."

We omit (not without regret) the beautiful picture of the sudden interference of Elizabeth to save her sinful lover from the Lynch law of the Bards ; and we have space only for a portion of her appeal against his being assassinated in the name of justice :

> " Oh, who that lives but hath within his heart
> Some cause to dread the suddenness of death ?
> And God is merciful : and suffers us,
> Even for our sins' sake ; and doth spare us time,
> Time to grow ready, time to take farewell !
> And sends us monitors and ministers—
> Old age, that steals the fullness from the veins ;
> And griefs, that take the glory from the eyes ;
> And pains, that bring us timely news of death :
> And tears, that teach us to be glad of him.
> For who can take farewell of all his sins
> On such a sudden summons to the grave ?
> Against high Heaven hath this man sinn'd, or you ?
> Oh, if it be against high Heaven, to Heaven
> Remit the compt ! lest, from the armoury
> Of The Eternal Justice ye pluck down,
> Heedless, that bolt The Highest yet withholds
> From his low-fallen head,—how fall'n ! how low !
> Yet not so fall'n, not so low-fallen, but what
> Divine Redemption, reaching everywhere,
> May reach at last even to this wretchedness,
> And, out of late repentance, raise it up
> With pardon unto peace."

The key note of the conclusion of the story is in these last lines. We will not pause over the exile substituted for the death of Tannhäuser :—

> " One lingering long look,
> Wild with remorse and vague with vast regrets,
> He lifted to Elizabeth. His thoughts
> Were then as those dumb creatures in their pain
> That make a language of a look."

and then :—

> " A fleeting darkness through the lurid arch ;
> A flying form along the glare beyond ;
> And he was gone."

How and when he returned—how she knelt,—

> " A faded watcher through the weary night,
> A meek sweet statue at the silver shrines,
> In deep, perpetual prayer for him she loved."

and what was the catastrophe of the story, it would be unfair to the authors to prevent the reader discovering for himself. It is enough to say that for very many years there has not been a more remarkable poem offered to the English public, who are never slow in proving that the cant cry that " poetry is a drug in the market," means simply that *bad* poetry is a drug in the market. Good poetry will be bought and read as long as there are hearts to feel and brains to understand. *Tannhaeuser* will be bought and read. The *anonyme* which the authors have adopted conceals names that would add an interest which the work itself does not need, and we predict, for the friends whose laurel wreaths are so inseparably intertwined, a bright future in the world of letters.

Should the severer judge deem that this is a poor criticism, which is all praise and no blame, we can only plead the story, from the Italian of Boccalini, told by Todd; narrating how a critic, having gathered together all the faults of an eminent poet, made a present of them to Apollo, who received them very graciously and resolved to make the critic a suitable return. This he did by setting the critic to divide the chaff and grain from a newly threshed sheaf of corn ; which task being performed, Apollo presented him with the chaff for his pains.

TANNHÄUSER.

This is the Land, the happy valleys these,

Broad breadths of plain, blue-vein'd by many a stream,

Umbrageous hills, sweet glades, and forests fair,

O'er which our good liege, Landgrave Herman, rules.

This is Thuringia: yonder, on the heights,

Is Wartburg, seat of our dear lord's abode,

Famous through Christendom for many a feat

Of deftest knights, chief stars of chivalry,

At tourney in its courts; nor more renown'd

For deeds of Prowess than exploits of Art,

Achieved when, vocal in its Muses' hall,   .

The minstrel-knights their glorious jousts renew,

And for the laurel wage harmonious war.

On this side spreads the Chase in wooded slopes

And sweet acclivities; and, all beyond,

The open flats lie fruitful to the sun

Full many a league ; till, dark against the sky,

Bounding the limits of our lord's domain,

The Hill of Hoersel rears his horrid front.

Woe to the man who wanders in the vast

Of those unhallow'd solitudes, if Sin,

Quickening the lust of carnal appetite,

Lurk secret in his heart : for all their caves

Echo weird strains of magic, direful-sweet,

That lap the wanton sense in blissful ease ;

While through the ear·a reptile music creeps,

And blandly-busy, round about the soul

Weaves its fell web of sounds.   The unhappy wight,

Thus captive made in soft and silken bands

Of tangled harmony, is led away—

Away adown the ever-darkening caves.

Away from fairness and the face of God,

Away into the mountain's mystic womb,

To where, reclining on her impious couch

All the fair length of her lascivious limbs,

Languid in light from roseate tapers flung,

Incensed with perfumes, tended on by fays,

The lustful Queen, waiting damnation, holds

Her bestial revels. The Queen of Beauty once,

A goddess call'd and worshipp'd in the days

When men their own infirmities adored,

Deeming divine who in themselves summ'd up

The full-blown passions of humanity.

Large fame and lavish service had she then,

Venus yclep'd, of all the Olympian crew

Least continent of Spirits and most fair.

So reap'd she honour of unwistful men,

Roman, or Greek, or dwellers on the plains

Of Egypt, or the isles to utmost Ind ;

Till came the crack of that tremendous Doom

That sent the false gods shivering from their seats,

Shatter'd the superstitious dome that blear'd

Heaven's face to man, and on the lurid world

Let in effulgence of untainted light.

As when, laid bare beneath the delver's toil

On some huge bulk of buried masonry

In hoar Assyria, suddenly reveal'd,

A chamber, gay with sculpture and the pomp

Of pictur'd tracery on its glowing walls,

No sooner breathes the wholesome heavenly air

Than fast its coloured bravery fades, and fall

Its ruin'd statues, crumbled from their crypts,

And all its gauds grow dark at sight of day ;

So darken'd and to dusty ruin fell

The fleeting glories of a Pagan faith,

Bared to Truth's influences bland, and smit

Blind by the splendours of the Bethlehem Dawn.

Then from their scatter'd temple in the minds

Of men, and from their long familiar homes,

Their altars, fanes, and shrines, the sumptuous seats

Of their mendacious oracles, out-slunk

The wantons of Olympus. ⸱ Forth they fled,

Forth from Dodona, Delos, and the depths

Of wooded Ida ; from Athenæ forth,

Cithæron, Paphos, Thebes, and all their groves

Of oak or poplar, dismally to roam

About the new-baptizèd earth ; exiled,

Bearing the curse, yet suffer'd for a space,

By Heaven's clear sapience and inscrutable ken,

To range the wide world, and assay their powers

To unregenerate redeem'd mankind :

If haply they by shadows and by shows,

2

Phantasmagoria, and illusions wrought

Of sight or sound by sorcery, may draw

Unwary men, or weak, into the nets

Of Satan their great Captain. She renown'd

'The fairest,' fleeing from her Cyprian isle,

Swept to the northwards many a league, and lodged

At length on Hörsel, into whose dark womb

She crept confounded. Thither soon she drew

Lewd Spirits to herself, and there abides,

Holding her devilish orgies ; and has power

With siren voices crafty to compel

Into her wanton home unhappy men

Whose souls to sin are prone. The pure at heart

Nathless may roam about her pestilent hill

Untainted, proof against perfidious sounds

Within whose ears an angel ever sings

Good tidings of great joy. Nor even they,

Whose hearts are gross, and who inflamed with lust

Enter, entrapp'd by sorceries, to her cave,

Are damn'd beyond redemption. For a while,

Slaves of their bodies, in the sloughs of Sin

They roll contented, wallowing in the arms

Of their libidinous goddess. But, ere long,

Comes loathing of the sensual air they breathe,

Loathing of light unhallow'd, sickening sense

Of surfeited enjoyment ; and their lips,

Spurning the reeky pasture, yearn for draughts

Of rock-rebounding rills, their eyes for sight

Of Heaven, their limbs for lengths of dewy grass :

What time sharp Conscience pricks them, and awake

Starts the requicken'd soul with all her powers,

And breaks, if so she will, the murderous spell,

Calling on God. God to her rescue sends

Voiced seraphims that lead the sinner forth

From darkness unto day, from foul embrace

Of that bloat Queen into the mother-lap

Of earth, and the caressent airs of Heaven;

Where he, by strong persistency of prayer,

By painful pilgrimage, by lengths of fast

That tame the rebel flesh, by many a night

Of vigil, days of deep repentant tears,

May cleanse his soul of her adulterate stains,

May from his sin-encrusted spirit shake

The leprous scales,—and, purely at the feet

Of his Redemption falling, may arise

Of Christ accepted.   Whoso doubts the truth,

Doubting how deep divine Compassion is,

Lend to my tale a willing ear, and learn.

Full twenty summers have fled o'er the land,

A score of winters on our Landgrave's head

Have shower'd their snowy honours, since the days

When in his court no nobler knight was known,

And in his halls no happier bard was heard,

Than bright Tannhäuser. Warrior, minstrel, he

Throve for a while within the general eye,

As some king-cedar, in Crusader tales,

The stateliest growth of Lebanonian groves :

For now I sing him in his matchless prime,

Not, as in latter days, defaced and marr'd

By secret sin, and like the wasted torch

Found in the dank grass at the ghastly dawn,

After a witches' revel. He was a man

In whom prompt Nature, as in those soft climes

Where life is indolently opulent,

Blossom'd unbid to graces barely won

From tedious culture, where less kindly stars

Cold influence keep ; and trothful men, who once

Look'd in his lordly, luminous eyes, and scann'd

His sinewous frame, compact of pliant power,

Aver he was the fairest-favour'd knight

That ever, in the light of ladies' looks,

Made gay these goodly halls. Oh! deeper·dole,

That so august a Spirit, sphered so fair,

Should from the starry sessions of his peers

Decline, to quench so bright a brilliancy

In Hell's sick spume. Ay me, the deeper dole!

From yonder tower the wheeling lapwing loves

Beyond all others, that o'ertops the pines,

And from his one white, wistful window stares

Into the sullen heart o' the land,—erewhile

The wandering woodman oft, at nightfall, heard

A sad, wild strain of solitary song

Float o'er the forest. Whoso heard it, paused

Compassionately, cross'd himself, and sigh'd

'Alas! poor Princess, to thy piteous moan

Heaven send sweet peace!' Heaven heard. And now
     she lies

Under the marble, 'mid the silent tombs,

Calm with her kindred ; as her soul above

Rests with the saints of God.

　　　　　　　The brother's child

Of our good lord the Landgrave was this maid,

And here with him abode ; for in the breach

At Ascalon her sire in Holy Land

Had fallen, fighting for the Cross.　These halls

Sheltered her infancy, and here she grew

Amŏng the shaggy barons, like the pale,

Mild-eyed March-violet of the North, that blows

Bleak under bergs of ice.　Full fair she grew,

And all men loved the rare Elizabeth ;

But she, of all men, loved one man the most,

Tannhäuser, minstrel, knight, the man in whom

All mankind flower'd.　Fairer growth, indeed,

Of knighthood never blossom'd to the eye ;

But, furl'd beneath that florid surface, lurk'd

A vice of nature, breeding death, not life ;

Such as where some rich Roman, to delight

Luxuriant days with labyrinthian walks

Of rose and lily, marble fountains, forms

Wanton of Grace or Nymph, and winding frieze

With sculpture rough, hath deck'd the summer haunts

Of his voluptuous villa,—there, festoon'd

With flowers, among the Graces and the Gods,

The lurking fever glides.

        A dangerous skill,

Caught from the custom of those troubadours

That roam the wanton South, too near the homes

Of the lost gods, had crept in careless use

Among our northern bards ; to play the thief

Upon the poets of a pagan time,

And steal, to purfle their embroider'd lays,

Voluptuous trappings of lascivious lore.

Hence had Tannhäuser, from of old, indulged

In song too lavish license to mislead

The sense among those fair but phantom forms

That haunt the unhallow'd past : wherefrom One Shape

Forth of the cloudy circle gradual grew

Distinct in dissolute beauty.   She of old,

Who from the idle foam uprose, to reign

In fancies all as idle,—that fair fiend,

Venus, whose temples are the veins in youth.

Now more and ever more she mix'd herself

With all his moods, and whisper'd in his walks ;

Or through the misty minster, when he kneel'd

Meek on the flint, athwart the incense-smoke

She stole on sleeping sunbeams, sprinkled sounds

Of cymbals through the silver psalms, and marr'd

His adoration : most of all, whene'er

He sought to fan those fires of holy love

That, sleeping oftenest, sometimes leapt to flame,

Kindled by kindred passion in the eyes

Of sweet Elizabeth, round him rose and roll'd

That miserable magic ; and, at times,

It drove him forth to wander in the waste

And desert places, there where prayerless man

Is most within the power of prowling fiends.

Time put his sickle in among the days.

Outcropp'd the coming harvest ; and there came

An evening with the Princess, when they twain

Together ranged the terrace that o'erlaps

The great south garden.   All her simple hair

A single sunbeam from the sleepy west

O'erfloated ; swam her soft blue eyes suffused

With tender ruth, and her meek face was moved

To one slow, serious smile, that stole to find

Its resting place on his.

                    Then, while he looked

On that pure loveliness, within himself

He faintly felt a mystery like pure love :

For through the arid hollows of a heart

Sered by delirious dreams, the dewy sense

Of innocent worship stole. The one great word

That long had hover'd in the silent mind

Now on the lip half settled ; for not yet

Had love between them been a spoken sound

For after speech to lean on ; only here

And there, where scatter'd pauses strew'd their talk,

Love seem'd to o'erpoise the silence, like a star

Seen through a tender trouble of light clouds.

But, in that moment, some mysterious touch,

A thought—who knows?—a memory—something caught

Perchance from flying fancies, taking form

Among the sunset clouds, or scented gusts

Of evening through the gorgeous glooms, shrunk up

His better angel, and at once awaked

The carnal creature sleeping in the flesh.

Then died within his heart that word of life

Unspoken, which, if spoken, might have saved

The dreadful doom impending.   So they twain

Parted, and nothing said : she to her tower,

There with meek wonder to renew the calm

And customary labour of the loom ;

And he into the gradual-creeping dark

Which now began to draw the rooks to roost

Along the windless woods.

                  His soul that eve

Shook strangely if some flickering shadow stole

Across the slopes where sunset, sleeping out

The day's last dream, yet linger'd low.   Old songs

Were sweet about his brain, old fancies fair

O'erflow'd with lurid life the lonely land :

The twilight troop'd with antic shapes, and swarm'd

Above him, and the deep mysterious woods

With mystic music drew him to his doom.

So rapt, with idle and with errant foot

He wander'd on to Hörsel, and those glades

Of melancholy fame, whose poisonous glooms,

Deck'd with the gleaming hemlock, darkly fringe

The Mount of Venus. There, a drowsy sense

Of languor seized him ; and he sat him down

Among a litter of loose stones and blocks

Of broken columns, overrun with weed,

Remnants of heathen work that sometime propp'd

A pagan temple.

Suddenly, the moon,

Slant from the shoulder of the monstrous hill,

Swung o'er a sullen lake, and softly touch'd

With light a shatter'd statue in the weed.

He lifted up his eyes, and all at once,

Bright in her baleful beauty, he beheld

The goddess of his dreams. Beholding whom,

Lost to his love, forgetful of his faith,

And fever'd by the stimulated sense

Of reprobate desire, the madman cried ;

' Descend, Dame Venus, on my soul descend!

Break up the marble sleep of those still brows

Where beauty broods!   Down all my senses swim,

As yonder moon to yonder love-lit lake

Swims down in glory !'

              Hell the horrid prayer

Accorded with a curse.   Scarce those wild words

Were utter'd, when like mist the marble moved,

Flusht with false life.   Deep in a slimy cloud

He seem'd to sink beneath the sumptuous face

Lean'd o'er him,—all the whiteness, all the warmth,

And all the luxury of languid limbs,

Where violet vein-streaks, lost in limpid lengths

Of snowy surface, wander faint and fine ;

Whilst cymbal'd music, stol'n from underneath,

Creeps through a throbbing light that grows and glows

From glare to greater glare, until it gluts

And gulfs him in.

      And from that hour, in court,

And chase, and tilted tourney, many a month,

From mass in holy church, and mirth in hall,

From all the fair assemblage of his peers,

And all the feudatory festivals,

Men miss'd Tannhäuser.

      At the first, as when

From some great oak his goodliest branch is lopp'd,

The little noisy birds, that built about

The foliage, gather in the gap with shrill

And querulous curiosity ; even so,

From all the twittering tongues that throng'd the court

Rose general hubbub of astonishment,

And vext surmise about the absent man :

Why absent? whither wander'd? on what quest

Of errant prowess?—for, as yet, none knew

His miserable fall.   But time wore on,

The wonder wore away; round absence crept

The weed of custom, and the absent one

Became at last a memory, and no more.

One heart within that memory lived aloof;

One face, remembering his, forgot to smile ;

Our Landgrave's niece the old familiar ways

Walk'd like a ghost with unfamiliar looks.

Time put his sickle in among the days.

The rose burn'd out; red autumn lit the woods ;

The last snows, melting, changed to snowy clouds ;

And Spring once more with incantations came

To wake the buried year.   Then did our liege,

Lord Landgrave Herman—for he loved his niece,

And.lightly from her simple heart had won

The secret of lost smiles, and why she droop'd

A wilted flower—thinking to dispel,

If that might be, her mournfulness, let cry

By heralds that, at coming Whitsuntide,

The minstrel-knights in Wartburg should convene

To hold high combat in the craft of song,

And sing before the Princess for the prize.

But, ere that time, it fell upon a day

When our good lord went forth to hunt the hart,

That he with certain of his court, 'mid whom

Was Wolfram,—once Tannhäuser's friend, himself

Among the minstrels held in high renown—

Came down the Wartburg valley, where they deem'd

To hold the hart at siege, and found him not:

But found, far down, at bottom of the glade,

Beneath a broken cross, a lonely knight

Who sat on a great stone, watching the clouds.

And Wolfram, being a little in the van

Of all his fellows, eager for the hunt,

Hurriedly ran to question of the knight

If he had view'd the hart.   But when he came

To parley with him, suddenly he gave

A shout of great good cheer ; for, all at once,

In that same knight he saw, and knew, though changed,

Tannhäuser, his old friend and fellow-bard.

Now, Wolfram long had loved Elizabeth

As one should love a star in heaven, who knows

The distance of it, and the reachlessness.

But when he knew Tannhäuser in her heart,

(For loving eyes in eyes beloved are swift

To search out secrets) not the less his own

Clave unto both ; and, from that time, his love

Lived like an orphan child in charity,

Whose loss came early, and is gently borne,

Too deep for tears, too constant for complaint.

And, therefore, in the absence of his friend

His inmost heart was heavy, when he saw

The shadow of that absence in the face

He loved beyond all faces upon earth.

So that when now he found that friend again

Whom he had miss'd and mourn'd, right glad was he

Both for his own and for the Princess' sake :

And ran and fell upon Tannhäuser's neck,

And all for joy constrain'd him to his heart,

Calling his fellows from the neighboring hills,

Who, crowding, came, great hearts and open arms

To welcome back their peer. The Landgrave then,

When he perceived his well-belovèd knight,

Was passing glad, and would have question'd him

Of his long absence. But the man himself

Could answer nothing ; staring with blank eyes

From face to face, then up into the blue

Bland heavens above ; astonied, and like one

Who, suddenly awaking out of sleep

After sore sickness, knows his friends again,

And would peruse their faces, but breaks off

To list the frolic bleating of the lamb

In far-off fields, and wonder at the world

And all its strangeness. ·Then, while the glad knights

Clung round him, wrung his hands, and dinn'd his ears

With clattering query, our fair lord himself

Unfolded how, upon the morrow morn,

There should be holden festive in his halls

High meeting of the minstrels of the land,

To sing before the Princess for the prize:

Whereto he bade him with ' O sir, be sure

There lives a young voice that shall tax your wit

To justify this absence from your friends.

We trust, at least, that you have brought us back

A score of giants' beards, or dragons' tails;

To lay them at the feet of our fair niece.

For think not, truant, that Elizabeth

Will hold you lightly quitted.'

                At that name,

Elizabeth, he started as a man

That hears on foreign shores, from alien lips,

Some name familiar to his fatherland ;

And all at once the man's heart inly yearns

For brooks that bubble, and for woods that wave

Before his father's door, while he forgets

The forms about him.   So Tannhäuser mused

A little space, then falter'd 'O my liege,

Fares my good lady well?—I pray my lord

That I may draw me hence a little while,

For all my mind is troubled : and, indeed,

I know not if my harp have lost his skill,

But, skill'd, or skilless, it shall find some tone

To render thanks to-morrow to my lord ;

To whose behests a bondsman, in so far

As my poor service holds, I will assay

To sing before the Princess for the prize.'

Then, on the morrow morn, from far and near

Flow'd in the feudatory lords.   The hills

Broke out ablaze with banners, and rung loud

With tingling trumpet notes, and neighing steeds.

For all the land, elate with lusty life,

Buzz'd like a beehive in the sun ; and all

The castle swarm'd from bridge to barbican

With mantle and with mail, whilst minster-bells

Rang hoarse their happy chimes, till the high noon

Clang'd from the towers.   Then, o'er the platform stoled

And canopied in crimson, lightly blew

The scepter'd heralds on the silver trump

Intense sonorous music, sounding in

The knights to hall.   Shrill clink'd the corridors

Through all the courts with clashing heels, or moved

With silken murmurs, and elastic sounds

Of lady laughters light ; as in they flow'd

Lord, Liegeman, Peer, and Prince, and Paladin,

And dame and damsel, clad in dimpling silk

And gleaming pearl ; who, while the groaning roofs

Re-echoed royal music, swept adown

The spacious hall, with due obeisance made

To the high dāis, and on glittering seats

Dropp'd one by one, like flocks of burnish'd birds

That settle down with sunset-painted plumes

On gorgeous woods.   Again from the outer wall

The intermitted trumpet blared ; and each

Pert page, a-tiptoe, from the benches lean'd

To see the minstrel-knights, gold-filleted,

That enter'd now the hall : Sir Mandeville,

The swan of Eisnach ; Wilfred of the Hills ;

Wolfram, surnamed of Willow-brook ; and next

Tanuhäuser, christen'd of the Golden Harp ;

With Walter of the Heron-chase ; and Max,

The seer : Sir Rudolf,. of the Raven-crest ;

And Franz, the falconer. They enter'd, each

In order, follow'd by a blooming boy

That bore his harp, and, pacing forward, bow'd

Before the Landgrave and Elizabeth.

Pale sat the Princess in her chair of state,

Perusing with fix'd eyes, that all belied

Her throbbing heart, the carven architrave,

Whereon the intricate much-vex'd design

Of leaf and stem disintertwined itself

With infinite laboriousness, at last

Escaping in a flight of angel forms ;

As tho' the carver's thought had been to show

The weary struggle of the soul to free

Her flight from earth's bewilderment, and all .

That frets her in the flesh.   But when, erewhile,

The minstrels enter'd, and Tannhäuser bow'd

Before the däis, the Landgrave at her side,

Saw, as he mused what theme to give for song,

The pallid forehead of Elizabeth

Flush to the fair roots of her golden hair,

And thought within himself: 'Our knight delays

To own a love that aims so near our throne ;

Hence, haply, this late absence from our court,

And those bewilder'd moods which I have mark'd :

But since love lightly catches, where it can,

At any means to make itself approved,

And since the singer may to song confide

What the man dares not trust to simple speech,

I, therefore, so to ease two hearts at once,

And signify our favour unto both,

Will to our well-beloved minstrels give

No theme less sweet than Love ; for, surely, he

That loves the best, will sing the best, and bear

The prize from all.' Therewith the Landgrave rose,

And all the murmuring Hall was hush'd to hear.

' O well-belovèd minstrels, in my mind

I do embrace you all, and heartily

Bid you a lavish welcome to these halls.

Oft have you flooded this fair space with song,

Waked these voiced walls, and vocal made yon roof,

As waves of surging music lapp'd against

Its resonant rafters.   Often have your strains

Ennobled souls of true nobility,

Rapt by your perfect pleadings in the cause

Of all things pure unto a purer sense

Of their exceeding loveliness.   No power

Is subtler o'er the spirit of man than Song—

Sweet echo of great thoughts, that, in the mind

Of him who hears congenial echoes waking,

Remultiplies the praise of what is good.

Song cheers the emulous spirit to the top

Of Virtue's rugged steep, from whence, all heights

Of human worth attain'd, the mortal may

Conjecture of God's unattainable,

Which is Perfection.—Faith, with her sisters twain

Of Hope and Charity, ye oft have sung,

And loyal Truth have lauded, and have wreathed

A coronal of music round the brows

Of stainless Chastity ; nor less have praised

High-minded Valour, in whose righteous hand

Burns the great sword of flaming Fortitude,

And have stirr'd up to deeds of high emprize

Our noble knights (yourselves among the noblest)

Whether on German soil for me, their prince,

Fighting, or in the Land of Christ for God.

Sing ye to-day another theme ; to-day

Within our glad society we see,

To fellowship of loving friends restored,

A long-missed face ; and hungerly our ears

Wait the melodious murmurs of a harp

That wont to feed them daintily.   What drew

Our singer forth, and led the fairest light

Of all our galaxy to swerve astray

From his fix'd orbit, and what now respheres,

After deflection long, our errant orb,

Implies a secret that the subtle power

Of Song, perchance, may solve.   Be then your theme

As universal as the heart of man,

Giving you scope to touch its deepest depths,

Its highest heights, and reverently to explore

Its mystery of mysteries.   Sing of Love :

Tell us, ye noble poets, from what source

Springs the prime passion ; to what goal it tends ;

Sing it how brave, how beautiful, how bright,

In essence how ethereal, in effect

How palpable, how human yet divine.

Up! up! loved singers, smite into the chords,

The lists are open'd, set your lays in rest,

And who of Love best chants the perfect praise,

Him shall Elizabeth as conqueror hail

And round his royal temples bind the bays.'

He said, and sat. And from the middle-hall

Four pages, bearers of the blazon'd urn

That held the name-scrolls of the listed bards,

Moved to Elizabeth. Daintily her hand

Dipp'd in the bowl, and one drawn scroll deliver'd

Back to the pages, who, perusing, cried :

'Sir Wolfram of the Willow-brook,—begin.'

Up-rose the gentle singer—he whose lays,

Melodious-melancholy, through the Land

Live to this day—and, fair obeisance made,

Assumed his harp and stood in act to sing.

Awhile, his dreamy fingers o'er the chords

Wander'd at will, and to the roof was turn'd

His meditative face ; till, suddenly,

A soft light from his spiritual eyes

Broke, and his canticle he thus began :

   ' Love among the saints of God,

    Love within the hearts of men,

    Love in every kindly sod

    That breeds a violet in the glen ;

    Love in heaven, and Love in earth,

    Love in all the amorous air ;

    Whence comes Love ? ah ! tell me where

    Had such a gracious Presence birth?

    Lift thy thoughts to Him, all-knowing,

    In the hallow'd courts above ;

    From His throne, for ever flowing,

    Springs the fountain of all Love :

Down to earth the stream descending

Meets the hills, and murmurs then,

In a myriad channels wending.

Through the happy haunts of men.

Blessèd ye, earth's sons and daughters,

Love among you flowing free ;

 Guard, oh! guard its sacred waters,

Tend on them religiously :

Let them through your hearts steal sweetly,   ·

With the spirit, wise and bland,

Minister unto them meetly,

Touch them not with carnal hand.

' Maiden, fashion'd so divinely,

Whom I worship from afar,

Smile thou on my soul benignly,

Sweet, my solitary star :

Gentle harbinger of gladness,

Still be with me on the way ;

Only soother of my sadness,

Always near, though far away :

Always near, since first upon me

Fell thy brightness from above,

And my troubled heart within me

Felt the sudden flow of Love ;

At thy sight that gushing river

Paused, and fell to perfect rest,

And the pool of Love for ever

Took thy image to its breast.

' Let me keep my passion purely,

Guard its waters free from blame,

Hallow Love, as knowing surely

It returneth whence it came :

From all channels, good or evil,

Love, to its pure source enticed,

Finds its own immortal level

In the charity of Christ.

Ye who hear, behold the river,

Whence it cometh, whither goes ;

Glory be to God the Giver,

From whose grace the fountain flows ;

Flows and spreads through all creation,

Counter-charm of every curse,

Love, the waters of Salvation,

Flowing through the universe !'

And still the rapt bard, though his voice had ceased,

And all the Hall had murmur'd into praise,

Pursued his plaintive theme among the chords,

Blending with instinct fine the intricate throng

Of thoughts that flow'd beneath his touch to find

Harmonious resolution.   As he closed,

Tannhäuser rising, fretted with delay,

Sent flying fingers o'er the strings, and sang :

' Love be my theme ! Sing her awake,

   My harp, for she hath tamely slept

   In Wolfram's song, a stagnant lake

   O'er which a shivering star hath crept.

' Awake, dull waters, from your sleep,

   Rise, Love, from thy delicious well,

   A fountain !—yea, but flowing deep

   With nectar and with hydromel ;

' With gurgling murmurs sweet, that teach

   My soul a sleep-distracting dream,

   Till on the marge I lie, and reach

   My longing lips towards the stream,

' Whose waves leap upwards to the brink,

   With drowning kisses to invite

   And drag me, willing, down to drink

   Delirious draughts of rare Delight.

'Who careless drink, as knowing well

The happy pastime, shall not tire,

For Love is inexhaustible,

And all-unfailing my Desire.

———————————

'Love's fountain-marge is fairly spread

With every incense-flower that blows,

With mossy sedge, and moss that grows

For fervid limbs a dewy bed ;

'And fays and fairies flit and wend

To keep the sweet stream flowing free,

And on Love's languid votary

The little elves delighted tend,

'And bring him honey-dews to sip,

Rare balms to cool him after play,

Or with sweet unguents smooth away

The kiss-crease on his ruffled lip ;

'And lilywhite his limbs they lave,

And roses in his cheeks renew,

That he, refresh'd, return to glue

His lips to Love's caressent wave,

'And feel, in that immortal kiss,

His mortal instincts die the death,

And human fancy fade beneath

The taste of unimagined bliss!

———————————

'Thus, gentle audience, since your ear

Best loves a metaphoric lay,

Of mighty Love I warble here

In figures, such as Fancy may :

'Now know ye how of Love I think

As of a fountain, failing never,

On whose soft marge I lie, and drink

Delicious draughts of Joy for ever.'

Abrupt he ceased, and sat.   And for a space,

No longer than the subtle lightning rests

Upon the sultry cloud at eventide,

The Princess smiled, and on her parted lips

Hung inarticulate applause ; but she

Sudden was ware that all the hall was mute

With blank disapprobation ; and her smile

Died, and vague fear was quicken'd in her heart

As Walter of the Heron-chase began :

    ' O fountain ever fair and bright,

      He hath beheld thee, source of Love,

      Who sung thee springing from above,

      Celestial from the founts of Light ;

    ' But he who from thy waters rare

      Hath thought to drain a gross delight,

      Blind in his spiritual sight,

      Hath ne'er beheld thee, fountain fair !

    ' Hath never seen the silver glow

      Of thy glad waves, crystalline clear,

      Hath never heard within his ear

      The music of thy murmurous flow.

' The essence of all Good thou art,
   Thy waters are immortal Ruth,
   Thy murmurs are the voice of Truth,
And music in the human heart :

' Thou yieldest faith that soars on high,
   And sympathy that dwells on earth ;
   The tender trust in human worth,
The hope that lives beyond the sky.

' Oh ! waters of the living Word,
   Oh ! fair vouchsafed us from above,
   Oh ! fountain of immortal Love,
What song of thee erewhile I heard !

' Learn, sacrilegious bard, from me
   How all ignoble was thy strain,
   That sought with trivial song to stain
The fountain of Love's purity ;

' That fountain thou hast never found,
   And should'st thou come with lips of fire
   To slake the thirst of brute Desire,
'Twould shrink and shrivel to the ground :

‘ Who seeks in Love’s pure stream to lave

His gross heart finds damnation near ;

Who laves in Love his spirit clear

Shall win Salvation from the wave.’

And now again, as when the plaintive lay

Of Wolfram warbled to harmonious close,

The crowd grew glad with plaudits ; and again

Tannhäuser, ruffled, rose his height, and smote

Rude in the chords his prelude of reply :

‘ What love is this that melts with Ruth,

Whose murmurs are the voice of Truth ?

Ye dazèd singers, cease to dream,

And learn of me your human theme :

Of that great Passion at whose feet

The vassal-world lies low,

Of Love the mighty, Love the sweet,

I sing, who reigns below ;

Who makes men fierce, tame, wild, or kind,

Sovran of every mood,

Who rules the heart, and rules the mind,

And courses through the blood :

Slave, of that lavish Power I sing,

Dispenser of all good,

Whose pleasure-fountain is the spring

Of sole beatitude.

' Sing ye of Love ye ne'er possess'd

In wretched tropes—a vain employment !

I sing the passion in my breast,

And know Love only in Enjoyment.'

To whom, while all the rustling hall was moved

With stormy indignation, stern up-rose,

Sharp in retort, Sir Wilfrid of the hills :

' Up, minstrels ! rally to the cry

Of outraged Love and Loyalty ;

Drive on this slanderer, all the throng,

And slay him in a storm of song.

Oh lecher ! shall I sing to thee

Of Love's untainted purity,

Of simple Faith, and tender Ruth,

Of Chastity and loyal Truth ?

As well sing Day's resplendent birth

To the blind mole that delves the earth

As seek from gross hearts, slough'd in sin,

Approval of pure Love to win !

Rather from thee I'll wring applause

For Love, the Avenger of his cause ;

Great Love, the chivalrous and strong,

To whose wide grasp all arms belong,

The lance, the battle-axe, and thong—

And eke the mastery in song.

' Love in my heart in all the pride

Of kinghood sits, and at his side,

To do the bidding of his lord,

Martial Valour holds the sword;

He strikes for Honour, in the name

Of Virtue and fair woman's fame,

And bids me shed my dearest blood

To venge aspersèd maidenhood:

Who soils her with licentious lie,

Him will I hew both hip and thigh,

Or in her cause will dearly die.

But thou, who in thy flashy song

Hast sought to do *all* Honour wrong,

Pass on—I will not stoop my crest

To smite thee, nor lay lance in rest.

Thy brawling words, of riot born,

Are worthy only of my scorn;

Thus at thy ears this song I fling,

Which in thy heart may plant its sting,

If ruin'd Conscience yet may wring

Remorse from such a guilty thing.'

Scarce from his lips had parted the last word

When, through the rapturous praise that rang around,

Fierce from his seat up-rising, red with rage,

With scornful lip, and contumelious eye,

Tannhäuser clang'd among the chords, and sang :

' Floutest thou me, thou grisly Bard ?

   Beware, lest I the just reward

   On thy puff'd insolence bestow,

   And cleave thee with my falchion's blow,—

   When I in song have laid thee low.

   I serve a Mistress mightier far

   Than tinkling rill, or twinkling star,

   And, as in my great Passion's glow

   Thy passion-dream will melt like snow,

   So I, Love's champion, at her call,

Will make thee shrink in field or hall,

And roll before me like a ball.

'Thou pauper-minded pedant dim,

Thou starveling-soul, lean heart and grim,

Wouldst thou of Love the praises hymn?

Then let the gaunt hyena howl

In praise of Pity; let the owl

Whoop the high glories of the noon, .

And the hoarse chough becroak the moon!

What canst thou prate of Love?   I trow

She never graced thy open brow,

Nor flush'd thy cheek, nor blossom'd fair

Upon thy parted lips; nor e'er

Bade unpent passion wildly start

Through the forced portals of thy heart

To stream in triumph from thine eye,

Or else delicious death to die

On other lips, in sigh on sigh.

' Of Love, dispenser of all bliss,

Of Love that crowns me with a kiss,

I here proclaim me champion-knight ;

And in her cause will dearly fight

With sword or song, in hall or plain,

And make the welkin ring again

With my fierce blows, or fervent strain.

But for such Love as thou canst feel,

Thou wisely hast abjured the steel,

Averse to lay thy hand on hilt,

Or in her honour ride a tilt :

Tame Love full tamely may'st thou jilt,

And keep bone whole, and blood unspilt.'

Outflash'd Sir Wilfrid's weapon, and outleapt

From every angry eye a thousand darts

Of unsheath'd indignation, and a shout

Went up among the rafters, and the Hall

Sway'd to and fro with tumult ; till the voice

Of our liege lord roared ' Peace !' and, 'midst the clang

Of those who parted the incensèd bards,

Sounded the harp of Wolfram.   Calm he stood,

He only calm of all the brawling crowd,

Which yet, as is its wont, contagion caught

From neighbouring nobleness, and a stillness fell

On all, and in the stillness soft he sang :

  ' Oh ! from your sacred seats look down,

   Angels and ministers of good ;

   With sanctity our spirits crown,

   And crush the vices of the blood !

  ' Open your hearts and set them free,

   That heavenly light may enter in ;

   And from this fair society

   Obliterate the taint of sin.

  ' Thee, holy Love, I bid arise

   Propitious to my votive lay ;

   Shine thou upon our darken'd eyes

   And lead us on the perfect way ;

' As, in the likeness of a Star,

Thou once arosest, guidance meet,

And led'st the sages from afar

To sit at holy Jesu's feet ;

' So guide us, safe from Satan's snares,

Shine out, sweet Star, around, above,

Till we have scaled the mighty stairs,

And reach'd thy mansions, Heavenly Love !'

Then, while great shouts went up of ' Give the prize

To Wolfram,' leapt Tannhäuser from his seat,

Fierce passion flaming from his lustrous orbs.

And, as a sinner, desperate to add

Depth to damnation by one latest crime,

Dies boastful of his blasphemies—even so,

Tannhäuser, conscious of the last disgrace

Incurr'd by such song in such company,

Intent to vaunt the vastness of his sin,

Thus, as in ecstacy, the song renewed :

'Goddess of Beauty, thee I hymn,

And ever worship at thy shrine;

Thou, who on mortal senses dim

Descending, makest man divine.

'Who hath embraced thee on thy throne,

And pastured on thy royal kiss,

He, happy, knows, and knows alone,

Love's full beatitude of bliss.

'Grim bards, of Love who nothing know,

Now cease the unequal strife between us;

Dare as I dared; to Hörsel go,·

And taste Love on the lips of Venus.'

Up-rose on every side and rustled down

The affrighted dames; and, like the shuddering crowd

Of particolour'd leaves that flits before

The gust of mid October, all at once

A hundred jewell'd shoulders, huddling, swept

The hall, and slanted to the doors, and fled

Before the storm, which now from shaggy brows

'Gan dart indignant lightnings. One alone

Of all that awe-struck womanhood remain'd,

The Princess. She, a purple hairbell frail,

That, swathed with whirlwind, to the bleak rock clings

When half a forest falls before the blast,

Rooted in utter wretchedness, and robed

In mockery of splendid state, still sat ;

Still watched the waste that widen'd in her life ;

And look'd as one that in a nightmare hangs

Upon the edge of horror, while from beneath

The creeping billow of humanity

Sprays all his hair with cold ; but hand or foot

He may not move, because the formless Fear

Gapes vast behind him.   Grief within the void

Of her stark eyes stood tearless : terror blanch'd

5

Her countenance ; and, over cloudy brows,

The shaken diamond made a restless light,

And trembled as the trembling star that hangs

O'er Cassiopeïa i' the windy north.

But now, from farthest end to end of all

The sullen movement swarming underneath,

Uproll'd deep hollow groans of growing wrath,

And, where erewhile in rainbow crescent ranged

The bright-eyed beauties of the court, fast throng'd

Faces inflamed with wrath, that rose and fell

Tumultuously gathering from between

Sharp-slanting lanes of steel.   For every sword

Flash'd bare upon a sudden : and over these,

Through the wide bursten doors the sinking sun

Stream'd lurid, lighting up that steely sea ;

Which, spotted white with foamy plumes, and ridged

With glittering iron, clash'd together and closed

About Tannhäuser.   Careless of the wrath

Roused by his own rash song, the singer stood ;

Rapt in remembrance, or by fancy fool'd

A visionary Venus to pursue,

With eyes that roam'd in rapture the blank air,

Until the sharp light of a hundred swords

Smote on the fatal trance, and scatter'd all

Its fervid fascination.   Swift from sheath

Then leapt the glaive and glitter'd in his hand,

And warily, with eye upon the watch,

Receding to the mighty main support

That, from the centre, propp'd the ponderous roof,

There, based against the pillar, fronting full

His sudden foes, he rested resolute,

Waiting assault.

But, hollow as a bell,

That tolls for tempest from a storm-clad tower,

Rang through the jangling shock of arms and men

The loud voice of the Landgrave.   Wide he swept

The solemn sceptre, crying 'Peace!' then said:

'Ye Lieges of Thuringia! whose just scorn,

In judgment sitting on your righteous brows,

Would seem to have forecast the dubious doom

Awaiting our decision ; ye have heard,

Not wrung by torture from reluctant lips,

Nor yet breathed forth with penitential pain

In prayer for pardon, nay, but rather fledged

And barb'd with boastful insolence, such a crime

Confest, as turns to burning coals of wrath

The dewy eyes of Pity, nor to Hope

One refuge spares, save such as rests perchance

Within the bounteous bosom of the Church ;

Who, caring for the frailty of her flock,

Holds mercy measureless as heaven is high.

Shuddering, ourselves have listen'd to what breaks

All bonds that bound to this unhappy man

The covenanted courtesies of knights,

The loyalties of lives by faith knit fast

In spiritual communion.   What behoves,

After deliberation, to award

In sentence, I to your high counsel leave,

Undoubting.   What may mitigate in aught

The weight of this acknowledged infamy

Weigh with due balance.   What to justice stern

Mild-minded mercy yet may reconcile

Search inly.   Not with rashness, not in wrath,

Invoking from the right hand of high God

His dread irrevocable angel, Death ;

Yet not unwary how one spark of hell,

If unextinguish'd, down the night of time

May, like the wreckers' beacon from the reefs,

Lure many to destruction : nor indeed

Unmindful of the doom by fire or steel

This realm's supreme tribunals have reserved

For those that, dealing in damnation, hold

Dark commerce with the common foe of man.

Weigh you in all its circumstance this crime :

And, worthily judging, though your judgment be

As sharp as conscience, be it as conscience clear.'

He ended: and a bitter interval

Of silence o'er the solemn hall congeal'd,

Like frost on a waste water, in a place

Where rocks confront each other,   Marshall'd round,

Black-bearded cheek and chin, with hand on heft,

Bent o'er the pommels of their planted swords,

A dreary cirque of faces ominous,

The sullen barons on each other stared

Significant.   As, ere the storm descends

Upon a Druid grove, the great trees stand

Looking one way, and stiller than their wont,

Until the thunder, rolling, frees the wind

That rocks them altogether ; even so,

That savage circle of grim-gnarlèd men,

Awhile in silence storing stormy thoughts,

Stood breathless; till a murmur moved them all,

And louder growing, and louder, burst at last

To a universal irrepressible roar

Of voices roaring, ' Let him die the death !'

And, in that roar released, a hundred swords

Rush'd forward, and in narrowing circle sloped

Sharp rims of shining horror round the doom'd,

Undaunted minstrel.   Then a piteous cry ;

And from the purple baldachin down sprang

The Princess, gleaming like a ghost, and slid

Among the swords, and standing in the midst

Swept a wild arm of prohibition forth.

Cowering, recoil'd the angry, baffled surge,

Leaving on either side a horrid ridge

Of rifted glare, as when the Red Sea waves

Hung heap'd and sunder'd, ere they roaring fell

On Egypt's chariots.   So there came a hush ;

And in the hush her voice, heavy with scorn :

' Or shall I call you men ? or beasts ? who seem

No nobler than the bloodhound and the wolf

Which scorn to prey upon their proper kind !

Christians I will not call you ! who defraud

That much-misapprehended holy name

Of reverence due by such a deed as, done,

Will clash against the charities of Christ,

And make a marr'd thing and a mockery

Of the fair face of Mercy.   You dull hearts,

And hard ! have ye no pity for yourselves ?

For man no pity ? man whose common cause

Is shamed and sadden'd by the stain that falls

Upon a noble nature !   You blind hands,

Thrust out so fast to smite a fallen friend !

Did ye not all conspire, whilst yet he stood

The stateliest soul among you, to set forth

And fix him in the foremost ranks of men?

Content that he, your best, should bear the brunt,

And head the van against the scornful fiend

That will not waste his weapons on the herd,

But saves them for the noblest.   And shall Hell

Triumph through you, that triumph in the shame

Of this eclipse that blots your brightest out,

And leaves you dark in his extinguish'd light?

Oh, who that lives but hath within his heart

Some cause to dread the suddenness of death?

And God is merciful; and suffers us,

Even for our sins' sake; and doth spare us time,

Time to grow ready, time to take farewell!

And sends us monitors and ministers—

Old age, that steals the fullness from the veins;

And griefs, that take the glory from the eyes;

And pains, that bring us timely news of death;

And tears, that teach us to be glad of him.

For who can take farewell of all his sins

On such a sudden summons to the grave?

Against high Heaven hath this man sinn'd, or you ?

Oh, if it be against high Heaven, to Heaven

Remit the compt! lest, from the armoury

Of The Eternal Justice ye pluck down,

Heedless, that bolt The Highest yet witholds

From this low-fallen head,—how fall'n ! how low!

Yet not so fall'n, not so low fall'n, but what

Divine Redemption, reaching everywhere,

May reach at last even to this wretchedness,

And, out of late repentance, raise it up

With pardon into peace.'

                    She paused : she touch'd,

As with an angel's finger, him whose pride

Obdurate now had yielded, and he lay,

Vanquish'd by Pity, broken at her feet.

She, lingering, waited answer, but none came

Across the silence.   And again she spake :

'Oh, not for him alone, and not for that

Which to remember now makes life for me

A wilderness of homeless griefs, I plead

Before you ; but, O Princes, for yourselves ;

For all that in your nobler nature stirs

To vindicate Forgiveness and enlarge

The lovely laws of Pity!   Which of you,

Here in the witness of all-judging God,

Stands spotless?   Which of you will boast himself

More miserably injured by this man

Than I, whose heart of all that lived in it

He hath untenanted?   Oh horrible!

Unheard of! from the blessèd lap of life

To send the soul, asleep in all her sins,

Down to perdition!   Be not yours the hands

To do this desperate wrong in sight of all

The ruthful faces of the Saints in Heaven.'

She passionately pleading thus, her voice

Over their hearts moved like that earnest wind

That, labouring long against some great night-cloud,

Sets free, at last, a solitary star,

Then sinks; but leaves the night not all forlorn

Ere the soft rain o'ercomes it.

                This long while

Wolfram, whose harp and voice were overborne

By burly brawlers in the turbulence

That shook that stormy senate, stood apart

With vainly-vigilant eye, and writhen hands,

All in mute trouble : too gentle to approve,

Too gentle to prevent, what pass'd : and still

Divided in himself 'twixt sharpest grief

To see his friend so fallen, and a drear

Strange horror of the crime whereby he fell.

So, like a headland light that down dark waves

Shines o'er some sinking ship it fails to save,

Look'd the pale singer down the lurid hall.

But when the pure voice of Elizabeth

Ceased, and clearlighted all with noble thoughts

Her face glow'd as an angel's, the sweet Bard,

Whose generous heart had scaled with that loved voice

Up to the lofty levels where it ceased,

Stood forth, and from the dubious silence caught

And carried up the purpose of her prayer ;

And drew it out, and drove it to the heart,

And clench'd it with conviction in the mind,

And fix'd it firm in judgment.   ·

                 From deep muse ·

The Landgrave started, toward Tannhäuser strode,

And, standing o'er him with an eye wherein

Salt sorrow and a moody pity gleam'd,

Spake hoarse of utterance :

                 ' Arise! go forth !

Go from us, mantled in the shames which make

Thee, stranger whom mine eye henceforth abhors,

The mockery of the man I loved, and mourn.

Go from these halls yet holy with the voice

Of her whose intercession for thy sake,—

If any sacred sorrow yet survive

All ruin'd virtues,—in remorse shall steep

The memory of her wrongs.   For thee remains

One hope, unhappiest! reject it not.   .

There goeth a holy pilgrimage to Rome,

Which not yet from the borders of our land.

Is parted ; pious souls and meek, whom thou

Haply may'st join, and of those holy hands,

Which sole have power to bind or loose, receive

Remission of thy sin.   For save alone

The hand of Christ's high Vicar upon earth

A hurt so heinous what may heal ?   What save

A soul so fall'n ?   Go forth upon thy ways,

Which are not ours : for we no more may mix

Congenial minds in converse sweet, no more

Together pace these halls, nor ever hear

Thy harp as once when all was pure and glad,

Among the days which have been.   All thy paths

Henceforth be paths of penitence and prayer,

Whilst over ours thy memory moving makes

A shadow, and a silence in our talk.

Get thee from hence, O all that now remains

Of one we honour'd!   Till the hand that holds

The keys of heaven hath oped for thee the doors

Of life in that far distance, let mine eye

See thee no more.   Go from us !'

                        Even then,

Even whilst he spake, like some sweet miracle,

From darkening lands that glimmer'd through the doors

Came, faintly heard along the filmy air

That bore it floating near, a choral chant

Of pilgrims pacing by the castle wall ;

And ' *salvum me fac Domine*' they sung

Sonorous, in the ghostly going out

Of the red-litten eve along the·land.

Then like a hand across the·heart of him

That heard it, moved that music from afar,

And beckon'd forth the better hope which leads

A man's life·up along the rugged road

Of high resolve. Tannhäuser moved, as moves·

The folded serpent smitten by the spring

And stirr'd with sudden sunlight, when he casts

His spotted skin, and renovated, gleams

With novel hues. One lingering long look,

Wild with remorse and vague with vast regrets,

He lifted to Elizabeth. His thoughts

Were then as those dumb creatures in their pain

That make a language of a look. He toss'd

Aloft his arms, and down to the great doors

With droop'd brows striding, groan'd 'To Rome! to Rome!'

Whilst the deep hall behind him caught the cry

And drove it clamorous after him, from all

Its hollow roofs reverberating ' Rome!'

A fleeting darkness thro' the lurid arch ;

A flying form along the glare beyond ;

And he was gone. The scowling Eve reach'd out

Across the hills a fiery arm, and took

Tannhäuser to her, like a sudden death.

So ended that great Battle of the Bards,

Whereof some rumour to the end of time

Will echo in this land.

                    And voided now

Of all his multitudes, the mighty Hall

Dumb, dismally dispageanted, laid bare

His ghostly galleries to the mournful moon ;

And night came down, and Silence, and the twain

Mingled beneath the starlight.   Wheel'd at will

The flitter-wingèd bat round lonely towers

Where, one by one, from darkening casements died

The taper's shine ; the howlet from the hills

Whoop'd : and Elizabeth, alone with Night

And Silence, and the Ghost of her slain youth,

Lay lost among the ruins of that day.

As when the buffeting gusts, that adverse blow

Over the Caribbean Sea, conspire

Conflicting breaths, and, savagely begot,

The fierce tornado rotatory wheels,

Or sweeps centripetal, or, all forces join'd,

Whirls circling o'er the madden'd waves, and they

Lift up their foaming backs beneath the keel

Of some frail vessel, and, careering high

Over a sunken rock, with a sudden plunge

Confound her,—stunn'd and strain'd, upon the peak

Poising one moment, ere she forward fall

To float dishelm'd, a wreck upon the waves :

So rose, engender'd by what furious blasts

Of passion, that fell hurricane that swept

Elizabeth to her doom, and left her now

A helmless hull upon the savage seas

Of life, without an aim, to float forlorn.

Longwhile, still shuddering from the shock that jarr'd

The bases of her being, piteous wreck

Of ruin'd hopes, upon her couch she lay,

Of life and time oblivious ; all her mind,

Lock'd in a rigid agony of grief,

Clasping, convulsed, its unwept woe ; her heart

Writhing and riven ; and her burthen'd brain

Blind with the weight of tears that would not flow.

But when, at last, the healing hand of Time

Had wrought repair upon her shatter'd frame ;

And those unskill'd physicians of the mind—

Importunate, fond friends, a host of kin—

Drew her perforce from solitude, she pass'd

Back to the world, and walk'd its weary ways

With dull mechanic motions, such as make

A mockery of life.   Yet gave she never,

By weeping or by wailing, outward sign

Of that great inward agony that she bore ;

For she was not of those whose sternest sorrow

Outpours in plaints, or weeps itself in dew ;

Not passionate she, nor of the happy souls

Whose grief comes temper'd with the gift of tears.

So, through long weeks and many a weary moon,

Silent and self-involved, without a sigh,

She suffer'd.   There, whence consolation comes,

She sought it—at the foot of Jesu's cross,

And on the bosom of the Virgin-spouse,

And in communion with the blessèd Saints.

But chief for him she pray'd whose grievous sin

Had wrought her desolation ; God besought

To touch the leprous soul and make it clean ;

And sued the Heavenly Pastor to recall

The lost sheep, wander'd from the pleasant ways,

Back to the pasture of the paths of peace.

So thrice a day, what time the blushing morn

Crimson'd the orient sky, and when the sun

Glared from mid-heaven or welter'd in the west,

Fervent she pray'd ; nor in the night forewent

Her vigils ; till at last from prayer she drew

A calm into her soul, and in that calm

Heard a low whisper—like the breeze that breaks

The deep peace of the forest ere the chirp

Of earliest birds salutes the advent Day—

Thrill through her, herald of the dawn of Hope.

Then most she loved from forth her leafy tower

Listless to watch the irrevocable clouds

Roll on, and daylight waste itself away

Along those dreaming woods, whence evermore

She mused, ' He will return ;' and fondly wove

Her webs of wistful fantasy till the moon

Was high in heaven, and in its light she kneel'd,

A faded watcher through the weary night,

A meek, sweet statue at the silver shrines,

In deep, perpetual prayer for him she loved.

And from the pitying Sisterhood of Saints

Haply that prayer shall win an angel down

To be his unseen minister, and draw

A drowning conscience from the deeps of Hell.

Time put his sickle in among the days.

Blithe Summer came, and into dimples danced

The fair and fructifying Earth, anon

Showering the gather'd guerdon of her play

Into the lap of Autumn ; Autumn stored

The gift, piled ready to the palsied hand

Of blind and begging Winter ; and when he

Closed his well-provender'd days, Spring lightly came

And scatter'd sweets upon his sullen grave.

And twice the seasons pass'd, the sisters three

Doing glad service for their hoary brother,

And twice twelve moons had wax'd and waned, and
    twice

The weary world had pilgrim'd round the sun,

When from the outskirts of the land there came

Rumour of footsore penitents from Rome

Returning, jubilant of remitted sins.

So chanced it, on a silent April eve

The westering sun along the Wartburg vale

Shot level beams, and into glory touch'd

The image of Madonna—where it stands

Hard by the common way that climbs the steep—

The image of Madonna, and the face

Of meek Elizabeth turn'd towards the Queen

Of Sorrows, sorrowful in patient prayer ;

When, through the silence and the sleepy leaves,

A breeze blew up the vale, and on the breeze

Floated a plaintive music.   She that heard,

Trembled ; the prayer upon her parted lips

Suspended hung, and one swift hand she press'd

Against the palpitating heart whose throbs

Confused the cunning of her ears.   Ah God!

Was this the voice of her returning joy?

The psalm of shriven pilgrims to their homes

Returning ?   Ay ! it swells upon the breeze

The ' *Nunc Dimittis*' of glad souls that sue

After salvation seen to part in peace.

Then up she sprung, and to a neighbouring copse

Swift as a startled hind, when the ghostly moon

Draws sudden o'er the silver'd heather-bells

The monstrous shadow of a cloud, she sped;

Pausing, low-crouch'd, within a maze of shrubs,

Whose emerald slivers fringed the rugged way

So broad, the pilgrim's garments as they passed

Would brush the leaves that hid her.   And anon

They came in double rank, and two by two,

With cumber'd steps, with haggard gait that told

Of bodily toil and trouble, with besoil'd

And tatter'd garments; natheless with glad eyes,

Whence look'd the soul disburthen'd of her sin,

Climbing the rude path, two by two they came.

And she, that watch'd with what intensest gaze

Them coming, saw old faces that she knew,

And every face turn'd skywards, while the lips

Pour'd out the heavenly psalm, and every soul

Sitting seraphic in the upturn'd eyes

With holy fervour rapt upon the song.

And still they came and pass'd, and still she gazed;

And still she thought, 'Now comes he!' and the chant

Went heavenwards, and the filèd pilgrims fared

Beside her, till their tale well-nigh was told.

Then o'er her soul a shuddering horror crept,

And, in that agony of mind that makes

Doubt more intolerable than despair,

With sudden hand she brushed aside the sprays,

And from the thicket lean'd and look'd.   The last

Of all the pilgrims stood within the ken

Of her keen gaze—save him all scann'd, and he

No sooner scann'd than cancell'd from her eyes

By vivid lids swept down to lash away

Him hateful, being other than she sought.

So for a space, blind with dismay, she paused,

But, he approaching, from the thicket leapt,

Clutch'd with wrung hands his robe, and gasp'd, 'The
    knight

'That with you went, returns not?' In his psalm

The fervid pilgrim made no pause, yet gazed

At his wild questioner, intelligent

Of her demand, and shook his head and pass'd.

Then she, with that mute answer stabb'd to the heart,

Sprung forward, clutch'd him yet once more, and cried,

'In Mary's name, and in the name of God,

Received the knight his shrift?' And, once again,

The pilgrim, sorrowful, shook his head and sigh'd,

Sigh'd in the singing of his psalm, and pass'd.

Then prone she fell upon her face, and prone

Within her mind Hope's shatter'd fabric fell—

The dear and delicate fabric of frail Hope

Wrought by the simple cunning of her thoughts,

That, labouring long, through many a dreamy day

And many a vigil of the wakeful night,

Piecemeal had rear'd it, patiently, with pain,

From out the ruins of her ancient peace.

O, ancient Peace ! that never shalt return ;

O, ruin'd Hope ! O, Fancy ! over-fond,

Futile artificer that build'st on air,

Marr'd is thy handiwork, and thou shalt please

With plastic fantasies her soul no more.

So lay she cold against the callous ground.

Her pale face pillow'd on a stone, her eyes

Wide open, fix'd into a ghastly stare

That knew no speculation ; for her mind

Was dark, and all her faculty of thought

Compassionately cancell'd.   But she lay

Not in the embrace of loyal Death, who keeps

His bride for ever, but in treacherous arms

Of Sleep that, sated, will restore to Grief

Her, snatch'd a sweet space from his cruel clutch.

So lay she cold against the callous ground,

And none was near to heed her, as the sun,

About him drawing the vast-skirted clouds,

Went down behind the western hill to die.

Now Wolfram, when the rumour reach'd his ears

That, from their quest of saving grace return'd,

The pilgrims all within the castle court

Were gather'd, flock'd about by happy friends,

Pass'd from his portal swiftly, and ran out

And join'd the clustering crowd. Full many a face,

Wasted and wan, he recogniz'd, and clasp'd

Full many a lean hand clutching at his own,

Of those who, stretch'd upon the grass, or propp'd

Against the boulder-stones, were press'd about

By weeping women, clamorous to unbind

Their sandal-thongs and bathe the bruisèd feet.

Then up and down, and swiftly through and through,

And round about, skirting the crowd, he hurried,

With greetings fair to all ; till, fill'd with fear,

Half-hopeless of his quest, yet harbouring hope,

He paused perplex'd beside the castle gates.

There, at his side, the youngest of the train,

A blue-eyed pilgrim tarried, and to him

Turn'd Wolfram questioning of Tannhäuser's fate ;

And learnt in few words how, his sin pronounced

Deadly and irremediable, the knight

Had faded from before the awful face

Of Christ's incensèd Vicar ; and none knew

Whither he wander'd, to what desolate lands,

Hiding his anguish from the eyes of men.

Then Wolfram groan'd, and clasp'd his hands, and cried

'Merciful God !' and fell upon his knees

In purpose as of prayer—but, suddenly,

About the gate the crowd moved, and a cry

Went up for space, when, rising, he beheld

Four maids who on a pallet bore the form

Of wan Elizabeth.   The whisper grew

That she had met the pilgrims, and had learn'd

Tannhäuser's fate, and fall'n beside the way.

And Wolfram, in the ghastly torchlight, saw

The white face of the Princess turn'd to his,

And for a space their eyes met ; then she raised

One hand towards Heaven, and smiled as who should say,

' O friend, I journey unto God ; farewell !'

But he could answer nothing ; for his eyes

Were blinded by his tears, and through his tears

Dimly, as in a dream, he saw her borne

Up the broad granite steps that wind within

The palace ; and his inner eye, entranced,

Saw in a vision four great Angels stand,

Expectant of her spirit at the foot

Of flights of blinding brilliancy of stairs

Innumerable, that through the riven skies

Scaled to the City of the Saints of God.

Then, when thick night fell on his soul, and all

The vision fled, he solitary stood

A crazèd man within the castle-court ;

Whence issuing, with wild eyes and wandering gait,

He through the darkness, groaning, pass'd away.

All that lone night, along the haunted hills,

By dizzy brinks of mountain precipices,

He fleeted, aimless as an unused wind

That wastes itself about a wilderness.

Sometimes from low brow'd caves, and hollow crofts

Under the hanging woods, there came and went

A voice of wail upon the midnight air,

As of a lost soul mourning ; and the voice

Was still the voice of his remember'd friend.

Sometimes (so fancy mock'd the fears she bred !)

He heard along the lone and eery land

Low demon laughters ; and a sullen strain

Of horror swell'd upon the breeze ; and sounds

Of wizard dance, with shawm and timbrel, flew

Ever betwixt waste air and wandering cloud

O'er pathless peaks. Then, in the distance toll'd,

Or seem'd to toll, a knell : the breezes dropp'd :

And, in the sudden pause, that passing bell

With ghostly summons bade him back return

To where, till dawn, a shade among the shades

Of Wartburg, watching one lone tower, he saw

A light that waned with all his earthly hopes.

The calm Dawn came and from the eastern cliff,

Athwart the glistening slopes and cold green copse,

Call'd to him, careless of a grief not hers ;

But he, from all her babbling birds, and all

Her vexing sunlight, with a weary heart

Drew close the darkness of the glens and glades

About him, flying through the forest deeps.

And day and night, dim eve and dewy dawn,

Three times returning, went uncared for by ;

And thrice the double twilights rose and fell

About a land where nothing seem'd the same,

At eve or dawn, as in the time gone by.

But, when the fourth day like a stranger slipp'd

To his unhonour'd grave, God's Angel pass'd

Across the threshold of the Landgrave's hall,

And in his bosom bore to endless peace

The weary spirit of Elizabeth.

Then in that hour when Death with gentle hand

Had droop'd the quiet eyelids o'er the eyes

That Wolfram lov'd, to Wolfram's heart there came

A calmness like the calmness of a grave

Wall'd safe from all the noisy walks of men

In some green place of peace where daisies grow.

His tears fell in the twilight with the dews,

Soft as the dews that with the twilight fell,

When, over scarr'd and weather-wounded walls,

Sharp-jaggèd mountain cones, and tangled quicks,

Eve's spirit, settling, laid the land to sleep

In skyey trance. Nor yet less soft to fuse

Memory with hope, and earth with heaven, to him,

Athwart the harsher anguish of that day,

There stole with tears the tender human sense

Of heavenly mercy. Through that milder mood,

Like waifs that float to shore when storms are spent,

Flow'd to his heart old memories of his friend

O'erwoven with the weed of other griefs—

Of other griefs for her that grieved no more,

And of that time when, like a blazing star

That moves and mounts between the Lyre and Crown,

Tannhäuser shone ; ere sin came, and with sin

Sorrow. And now if yet Tannhäuser lived

None knew : and if he lived, what hope in life ?

And if he lived no more, what rest in death?

But every way the dreadful doom of sin.

Thus musing much on all the mystery

Of life, and death, and love that will not die,

He wander'd forth, incurious of the way ;

Which took the wont of other days, and wound

Along the valley.   Now the nodding star

Of even, and the deep the dewy hour

Held all the sleeping circle of the hills ;

Nor any cloud the stainless heavens obscured,

Save where, o'er Höersel folded in the frown

Of all his wicked woods, a fleecy fringe

Of vapour veil'd the slowly sinking moon.

There, in the shade, the stillness, o'er his harp

Leaning, of love, and life, and death he sang

A song to which from all her aëry caves

The mountain echo murmur'd in her sleep.

But, as the last strain of his solemn song

Died off among the solitary stars,

There came in answer from the folded hills

A note of human woe. He turn'd, he look'd

That way the sound came o'er the lonely air ;

And, seeing, yet believed not that he saw,

But, nearer moving, saw indeed hard-by,

Dark in the darkness of a neighbouring hill,

Lying among the splinter'd stones and stubs

Flat in the fern, with limbs diffused as one

That, having fallen, cares to rise no more,

A pilgrim ; all his weeds of pilgrimage

Hanging and torn, his sandals stain'd with blood

Of bruisèd feet, and, broken in his hand,

His wreathèd staff.

          And Wolfram wistfully

Look'd in his face, and knew it not. ' Alas !

Not him,' he murmur'd, 'not my friend!'   And then,

'What art thou, pilgrim? whence thy way? how fall'n

In this wild glen? at this lone hour abroad

When only Grief is stirring?'   Unto whom

That other, where he lay in the long grass,

Not rising, but with petulant gesture, 'Hence!

Whate'er I am, it skills not.   Thee I know

Full well, Sir Wolfram of the Willow-brook,

The Well-belovèd Singer!'

                              Like a dart

From a friend's hand that voice thro' Wolfram went:

For memory over all the ravaged form

Wherefrom it issued, wandering, fail'd to find

The man she mourn'd ; but Wolfram, to the voice

No stranger, started smit with pain, as all

The past on those sharp tones came back to break

His heart with hopeless knowledge.   And he cried,

'Alas, my brother!'   Such a change, so drear,

In all so unlike all that once he was

Show'd the lost knight Tannhäuser, where he lay

Fallen across the split and morsell'd crags

Like a dismantled ruin.   And Wolfram said,

'O lost! how comest thou, unabsolved, once more

Among these valleys visited by death,

And shadow'd with the shadow of thy sin?'

Whereto in scorn Tannhäuser, 'Be at rest

O fearful in thy righteousness! not thee,

Nor grace of thine, I seek.'

            Speaking, he rose

The spectre of a beauty waned away ;

And, like a hollow echo of himself

Mocking his own last words, he murmur'd, 'Seek!

Alas! what seek I here, or anywhere?

Whose way of life is like the crumbled stair

That winds and winds about a ruin'd tower,

And leads no-whither!'

But Wolfram cried, 'Yet turn !

For, as I live, I will not leave thee thus.

My life shall be about thee, and my voice

Lure scared Hope back to find a resting-place

Even in the jaws of Death.   I do adjure thee,

By all that friendship yet may claim, declare

That, even though unabsolved, not uncontrite,

Thy soul no more hath lapsed into the snare

Of that disastrous sorcery.   Bid me hail,

Seen through the darkness of thy desolation,

Some light of purer purpose ; since I deem

Not void of purpose hast thou sought these paths

That range among the places of the past ;

And I will make defeat of Grief with such

True fellowship of tears as shall disarm

Her right hand of its scorpions ; nor in vain

My prayers with thine shall batter at the gates

Of Mercy, through all antagonisms of fate

Forcing sharp inlet to her throne in Heaven.'

Whereat Tannhäuser, turning tearless eyes

On Wolfram, murmur'd mournfully, 'If tears

Fiery as those from fallen seraphs distill'd,

Or centuries of prayers for pardon sigh'd

Sad, as of souls in purgatorial glooms,

Might soften condemnation, or restore

To her, whom most on earth I have offended,

The holy freight of all her innocent hopes

Wreck'd in this ruin'd venture, I would weep

Salt oceans from these eyes. But I no more

May drain the deluge from my heart, no more

On any breath of sigh or prayer rebuild

The rainbow of discovenanted Hope.

Thou, therefore, Wolfram—for her face, when mine

Is dark for ever, thine eyes may still behold—

Tell her, if thou unblamed may'st speak of one

Sign'd cross by the curse of God and cancell'd out,

How, at the last, though in remorse of all

That makes allegiance void and valueless,

To me has come, with knowledge of my loss,

Fealty to that pure passion, once betray'd,

Wherewith I loved, and love her.'

                              There his voice,

Even as a wave that, touching on the shore

To which it travell'd, is shiver'd and diffused,

Sank, scattered into spray of wasteful sighs,

And back dissolved into the deeper grief.

To whom, Wolfram, ' O answer by the faith

In which mankind are kindred, art thou not

From Rome, unhappiest?' ' From Rome? ah me!'

He mutter'd, ' Rome is far off, very far,

And weary is the way!' But undeterr'd

Wolfram renew'd, ' And hast thou not beheld

The face of Christ's High Vicar?'   And again,

' Pass on,' he mutter'd, ' what is that to thee ?'

Whereto, with sorrowful voice, Wolfram, ' O all,

And all in all to me that love my friend!'

' My friend!' Tannhäuser laugh'd a bitter laugh.

Then sadlier said, 'What thou would'st know, once known,

Will cause thee to recall that wasted word

And cancel all the kindness in thy thoughts ;

Yet shalt thou learn my misery, and learn

The man so changed, whom once thou calledst "friend,"

That unto him the memory of himself

Is as a stranger.'   Then, with eyes that swam

True sorrow, Wolfram stretch'd his arms and sought

To clasp Tannhäuser to him : but the other

Waved him away, and with a shout that sprang

Fierce with self-scorn from misery's deepest depth,

'Avaunt!' he cried, 'the ground whereon I tread,

Is ground accurst!

   'Yet stand not so far off

But what thine ears, if yet they will, may take

The tale thy lips from mine have sought to learn ;

Then, sign thyself, and peaceful go thy ways.'

And Wolfram, for the grief that choked his voice,

Could only murmur 'Speak!' But for a while

Tannhäuser to sad silence gave his heart ;

Then fetch'd back some far thought, sighing, and said :

'O Wolfram, by the love of lovelier days

Believe I am not so far fallen away

From all I was while we might yet be friends,

But what these words, haply my last, are true :

True as my heart's deep woe what time I felt

Cold on my brow tears wept, and wept in vain,

For me, among the scorn of alter'd friends,

Parting that day for Rome.   Remember this :

That when, in the after years to which I pass

A by-word, and a mockery, and no more,

Thou, honour'd still by honourable men,

Shalt hear my name dishonour'd, thou may'st say,

" Greatly he grieved for that great sin he sinn'd."

' Ever, as up the windy alpine way,

We halting oft by cloudy convent doors,

My fellow pilgrims warm'd themselves within,

And ate and drank, and slept their sleep, all night

I, fasting, slept not ; but in ice and snow

Wept, aye remembering her that wept for me,

And loathed the sin within me.   When at length

Our way lay under garden terraces

Strewn with their dropping blossoms, thick with scents,

Among the towers and towns of Italy,

What sumptuous airs along them, like the ghosts

Of their old gods, went sighing, I nor look'd

Nor linger'd, but with bandaged eyeballs prest,

Impatient, to the city of the shrine

Of my desired salvation. There by night

We enter'd. There, all night, forlorn I lay

Bruised, broken, bleeding, all my garments torn,

And all my spirit stricken with remorse

Prostrate beneath the great cathedral stairs.

So the dawn found me. From a hundred spires

A hundred silvery chimes rang joy : but I

Lay folded in the shadow of my shame,

Darkening the daylight from me in the dust.

Then came a sound of solemn music flowing

To where I crouch'd ; voices and trampling feet :

And, girt by all his crimson cardinals,

In all his pomp the sovran Pontiff stood

Before me in the centre of my hopes ;

Which trembled round him into glorious shapes,

Golden, as clouds that ring the risen sun.

And all the people, all the pilgrims, fell

Low at his sacred feet, confess'd their sins,

And, pardon'd, rose with psalms of jubilee

And confident glad faces.

     ' Then I sprang

To where he paused above me ; with wild hands

Clutch'd at the skirts I could not reach ; and sank

Shiveringly back ; crying, " O holy, and high,

And terrible, thou hast the keys of heaven !

Thou that dost bind and dost unloose, from me,

For Mary's sake, and the sweet Saints, unbind

The grievous burden of the curse I bear." '

And when he question'd, and I told him all

The sin that smoulder'd in my blood, how bred,

And all the strangeness of it, then his face

Was as the Judgment Angel's ; and I hid

My own ; and, hidden from his eyes, I heard :

' " Hast thou within the nets of Satan lain ?

Hast thou thy soul to her perdition pledged ?

Hast thou thy lip to Hell's Enchantress lent,

To drain damnation from her reeking cup?

Then know that sooner from the wither'd staff

That in my hand I hold green leaves shall spring,

Than from the brand in hell-fire scorch'd rebloom

The blossoms of salvation."

        ' The voice ceased,

And, with it all things from my sense. I waked

I know not when, but all the place was dark : .

Above me, and about me, and within

Darkness : and from that hour by moon or sun

Darkness unutterable as of death

Where'er I walk. But death himself is near !

Oh, might I once more see her, unseen ; unheard,

Hear her once more ; or know that she forgives

Whom Heaven forgives not, nor his own lost peace ;

I think that even among the nether fires

And those dark fields of Doom to which I pass,

Some blessing yet will haunt me.'

             Sorrowfully

He rose among the tumbled rocks and lean'd

Against the dark. As one that many a year,

Sunder'd by savage seas unsociable

From kin and country, in a desert isle

Dwelling till half dishumaniz'd, beholds

Haply, one eve, a far-off sail go by,

That brings old thoughts of home across his heart ;

And still the man who thinks—'They are all gone,

Or changed, that loved me once, and I myself

No more the same'—watches the dwindling speck

With weary eyes, nor shouts, nor waves a hand ;

But after, when the night is left alone,

A sadness falls upon him, and he feels

8

More solitary in his solitudes,

And tears come starting fast ; so, tearful, stood

Tannhäuser, whilst his melancholy thoughts,

From following up far-off a waning hope,

Back to himself came, one by one, more sad

Because of sadness troubled.

           Yet not long

He rested thus ; but murmur'd, ' Now, farewell !

I go to hide me darkly in the groves

That she was wont to haunt ; where some sweet chance

Haply may yield me sight of her, and I

May stoop, she pass'd away, to kiss the ground

Made sacred by her passage ere I die.'

But him departing Wolfram held, ' Vain ! vain !

Thy footstep sways with fever, and thy mind

Wavers within thy restless eyes. Lie here,

O unrejected, in my arms, and rest !'

Now o'er the cumbrous hills began to creep

A thin and watery light : a whisper went

Vague through the vast and dusky-volumed woods :

And, uncompanion'd, from a drowsy copse

Hard-by a solitary chirp came cold :

While, spent with inmost trouble, Tannhäuser lean'd

His wan cheek pillow'd upon Wolfram's breast,

Calm, as in death, with placid lips down lock'd.

And Wolfram pray'd within his heart, ' Ah, God !

Let him not die, not yet, not thus, with all

The sin upon his spirit !' But while he pray'd

Tannhäuser raised delirious looks, and sigh'd,

' Hearest thou not the happy songs they sing me ?

Seëst thou not the lovely floating forms ?

O fair, and fairer far than fancy fashion'd !

O sweet the sweetness of the songs they sing !

For thee . . . they sing . . . the goddess waits : for thee

With braided blooms the balmy couch is strewn,

And loosed for thee... they sing *...the golden zone.*

Fragrant for thee the lighted spices fume

With streaming incense sweet, and sweet for thee

The scatter'd rose, the myrtle crown, the cup,

The nectar cup for thee !... they sing.   *Return,*

Though late, too long desired,... I hear them sing,

Delay no more delights too long delay'd :

Turn to thy rest;... they sing *...the married doves*

Murmur; the Fays soft-sparkling tapers tend ;

The odours burn the purple bowers among ;

And Love for thee, and Beauty, waits !... they sing.'

'Ah me! ah madman!' Wolfram cried, ' yet cram

Thy cheated ears, nor chase with credulous heart

The fair dissembling of that dream.   For thee

Not roses now, but thorns ; nor myrtle wreath,

But cypress rather and the graveyard flower

Befitting saddest brows ; nor nectar pour'd,

But prayers and tears! For thee in yonder skies

An Angel strives with Sin and Death ; for thee

Yet pleads a spirit purer than thine own :

For she is gone! gone to the breast of God!

Thy Guardian Angel while she walk'd the earth,

Thine intercessionary Saint while now

For thee she sues about the Throne of Thrones,

Beyond the stars, our star, Elizabeth !'

Then Wolfram felt the shatter'd frame that lean'd

Across his breast with sudden spasms convulsed.

'Dead! is she dead?' Taunhäuser murmur'd, ' dead !

Gone to the grave, so young! murder'd—by me !

Dead—and by my great sin! O Wolfram, turn

Thy face from mine.   I am a dying man !'

And Wolfram answer'd, ' Dying ? ah, not thus!

' Yet make one sign thou dost repent the past,

One word, but one ! to say thou hast abhorr'd

The false she devil that, with her damnèd charms,

Hath wrought this ruin ; and I, though all the world

Roar out against thee, aye ! though fiends of hell

Howl from the deeps, yet I, thy friend, even yet

Will cry them " Peace!" and trust the hope I hold

Against all desperate odds, and deem thee saved.'

Whereto Tannhäuser, speaking faintly, ' Friend,

The fiend that haunts in ruins through my heart

Will wander sometimes. In the nets I trip,

When most I fret the meshes. These spent shafts

Are of a sickly brain that shoots awry,

Aiming at something better. Bear with me.

I die : I pass I know not whither : yet know

That I die penitent. O Wolfram, pray,

Pray for my soul ! I cannot pray myself.

I dare not hope : and yet I would not die

W thout a hope, if any hope, though faint

And far beyond this darkness, yet may dwell

In the dear death of Him that died for all.'

He whispering thus ; far in the Aurorean East

The ruddy sun, uprising, sharply smote

A golden finger on the airy harps

By Morning hung within her leafy bowers ;

And all about the budded dells, and woods

With sparkling-tassell'd tops, from birds and brooks

A hundred hallelujahs hail'd the light.

The whitethorn glisten'd from the wakening glen :

O'er golden gravel danced the dawning rills :

All the delighted leaves by copse and glade

Gamboll'd ; and breezy bleatings came from flocks

Far off in pleasant pastures fed with dew.

But whilst, unconscious of the silent change

Thus stol'n around him, o'er the dying bard

Hung Wolfram, on the breeze there came a sound

Of mourning moving down the narrow glen ;

And, looking up, he suddenly was ware

Of four white maidens, moving in the van

Of four black monks who bore upon her bier

The flower-strewn corpse of young Elizabeth.

And after these, from all the castled hills,

A multitude of lieges and of lords ;

A multitude of men at arms, with all

Their morions hung with mourning ; and in midst,

His worn cheek channell'd with unwonted tears,

The Landgrave, weeping for Elizabeth.

These, as the sad procession nearer wound,

And nearer, trampling bare the feathery weed

To where Sir Wolfram rested o'er his friend,

Tannhäuser caught upon his dying gaze ;

And caught, perchance, upon the inward eye,

Far, far beyond the corpse, the bier, and far

Beyond the widening circle of the sun,

Some sequel of that vision Wolfram saw :

The crownèd Spirit by the Jasper Gates ;

The four white Angels o'er the walls of Heaven ;

The shores where, tideless, sleep the seas of Time

Soft by the City of the Saints of God.

Forth, with the strength that lastly comes to break

All bonds, from Wolfram's folding arm he leapt,

Clamber'd the pebbly path, and, groaning fell

Flat on the bier of love—his bourn at last !

Then, even then, while question question chased

About the ruffled circle of that grief,

And all was hubbub by the bier, a noise

Of shouts and hymns brake in across the hills,

That now o'erflow'd with hurrying feet ; and came,

Dash'd to the hip with travel, and dew'd with haste,·

A flying post, and in his hand he bore

A wither'd staff o'erflourish'd with green leaves ;

Who,—follow'd by a crowd of youth and eld,

That sang to stun with sound the lark in heaven,

' A miracle! a miracle from Rome!

Glory to God that makes the bare bough green!'—

Sprang in the midst, and, hot for answer, ask'd

News of the Knight Tannhäuser.

                    Then a monk

Of those that, stoled in sable, bore the bier

Pointing, with sorrowful hand, ' Behold the man!'

But straight the other, ' Glory be to God!

This from the Vicar of the fold of Christ :

The wither'd staff hath flourish'd into leaves,

The brand shall bloom, though burn'd with fire, and thou

—Thy soul from sin be saved!'   To whom, with tears

That flash'd from lowering lids, Wolfram replied :

' To him a swifter message, from a source

Mightier than whence thou comest, hath been vouchsafed.

See these stark hands, blind eyes, and bloodless lips,

This shatter'd remnant of a once fair form,

Late home of desolation, now the husk

And ruin'd chrysalis of a regal spirit

That up to heaven hath parted on the wing !

But thou, to Rome returning with hot speed,

Tell the high Vicar of the Fold of Christ

How that lost sheep his rescuing hand would reach,

Although by thee unfound, is found indeed,

And in the Shepherd's bosom lies at peace.'

And they that heard him lifted up the voice

And wept.   But they that stood about the hills

Far off, not knowing, ceased not to cry out,

' Glory to God that makes the bare bough green !'

Till Echo, from the inmost heart of all

That mellowing morn blown open like a rose

To round and ripen to the perfect noon,

Resounded, ' Glory ! glory !' and the rocks

From glen to glen rang ' Glory unto God !'

And so those twain, sever'd by Life and Sin,

By Love and Death united, in one grave

Slept.   But Sir Wolfram pass'd into the wilds :

There, with long labour of his hands, he hew'd

A hermitage from out the hollow rock,

Wherein he dwelt a solitary man.

There, many a year, at nightfall or at dawn,

The pilgrim paused, nor ever paused in vain,

For words of cheer along his weary way.

But once, upon a windy night, men heard

A noise of rustling wings, and at the dawn

They found the hermit parted to his peace.

The place is yet.   The youngest pilgrim knows,

And loves it.   Three grey rocks ; and, over these,

A mountain ash that, mourning, bead by bead,

Drops her red rosary on a ruin'd cell.

———————

So sang the Saxon Bard.   And when he ceased,

The women's cheeks were wet with tears ; but all

The broad-blown Barons roar'd applause, and flow'd

The jostling tankards prodigal of wine.

THE END.

S. H. GOETZEL & CO.'S
LIST OF PUBLICATIONS.

————•◆•——

THE WAR IN NICARAGUA, written by Gen. WILLIAM WALKER.
One vol. 12mo., Cloth, complete, $1 50; do. Half Calf, $2 50.

SONGS AND POEMS OF THE SOUTH, by Hon. A. B. MEEK.
One vol. 12mo., Cloth, $1 00 ; do. Gilt, $1 25 ; do. Morocco extra, $2 50.

ROMANTIC PASSAGES IN SOUTH-WESTERN HISTORY,
By Hon. A. B. MEEK. One vol. 12mo. Cloth, $1 25.

THE RED EAGLE, by Hon. A. B. MEEK. One volume 8vo.,
Cloth, $1 00.

CODE OF ORDINANCES FOR THE CITY OF MOBILE, by
Hon. ALEXANDER McKINSTRY. One vol. 8vo., Sheep, $4 00.

REV. DR. P. P. NEELEY'S SERMONS. One vol. 12mo.
Cloth, $1 25.

SOUVENIRS OF TRAVEL, by M'ME OCTAVIA WALTON LEVERT,
Two vols. 12mo. Cloth, $2 00; Cloth Gilt, $2 50; Half Morocco Gilt, $4 00;
Turkey Morocco Antique, $5 00.

THE DISCOVERY OF FRANKLIN, by J. J. TURNER. One vol.
12mo. cloth, 60 cents.

HORIZONTAL PLOWING AND HILL-SIDE DITCHING, by
Dr. N. T. SORSBY, of Alabama. One vol. paper, 50 cents.

ELLEN; OR THE FANATIC'S DAUGHTER, by MRS. N. G.
COWDIN. One vol. 12mo. cloth, $1 25.

HARDEE'S RIFLE AND INFANTRY TACTICS. Two vols.
24mo. $3 00.

A STRANGE STORY, by Sir E. BULWER LYTTON, 1 v. paper, $2 50.

GREAT EXPECTATIONS, by CHARLES DICKENS, (in press) $2 50.

———

☞ Orders from abroad are respectfully requested to give *Distinct Directions* of their
Postoffices, Landings or Railroad Stations.

S. H. GOETZEL & CO., Mobile, Ala.

www.ingramcontent.com/pod-product-compliance
Lightning Source LLC
Chambersburg PA
CBHW030619270326
41927CB00007B/1237